JOHN RUTTER
FEEL THE SPIRIT

A CYCLE OF SPIRITUALS

FOR MEZZO-SOPRANO SOLO,
MIXED CHOIR, AND ORCHESTRA
OR CHAMBER ENSEMBLE

CONTENTS

MUSIC DEPARTMENT

OXFORD
UNIVERSITY PRESS

Feel the Spirit is available in two different instrumentations:

1. **Full orchestra**
   2 flutes
   2 oboes (oboe 2 doubling cor anglais)
   2 clarinets in A and B flat
   Bass clarinet
   2 bassoons
   4 horns in F
   3 trumpets in B flat
   3 trombones (2 tenor, 1 bass)
   Tuba
   Timpani (3 pedal timpani)
   Percussion (2 players: glockenspiel, suspended cymbal, clash cymbals,
   tambourine, claves, bass drum, drum kit)
   Harp
   Strings (1st and 2nd violins, violas, celli, basses)

2. **Chamber ensemble**
   Flute
   Oboe (doubling cor anglais)
   Clarinet in B flat (doubling bass clarinet)
   Bassoon
   Horn in F
   Trumpet in B flat
   Timpani (optional) and percussion (1 player: glockenspiel, suspended cymbal,
   clash cymbals, tambourine, claves, drum kit)
   Harp
   *Violin 1
   *Violin 2
   *Viola
   *Cello
   *Bass

*One or more players on each part.

Scores and parts are available on rental from Oxford University Press or its appointed agent.

> *Feel the Spirit* was first performed on 17th June 2001 in Carnegie Hall, New York, by Melanie Marshall (mezzo-soprano), the New England Symphonic Ensemble (director: Virginia-Gene Rittenhouse), and participating choirs in a MidAmerica Productions concert (Music Director and General Director: Peter Tiboris). The conductor was John Rutter.
>
> *Feel the Spirit* has been recorded by Melanie Marshall and the Cambridge Singers, with the BBC Concert Orchestra, conducted by John Rutter. The recording is on the Collegium label (CSCD 523).

Duration: 30 minutes

FEEL THE SPIRIT

arranged by
JOHN RUTTER

1. Joshua fit the battle of Jericho

OXFORD UNIVERSITY PRESS MUSIC DEPARTMENT, GREAT CLARENDON STREET, OXFORD OX2 6DP

'Go   blow those   ram horns' Josh - ua   cried,   'Cos the

_____ with   spear in   hand:__

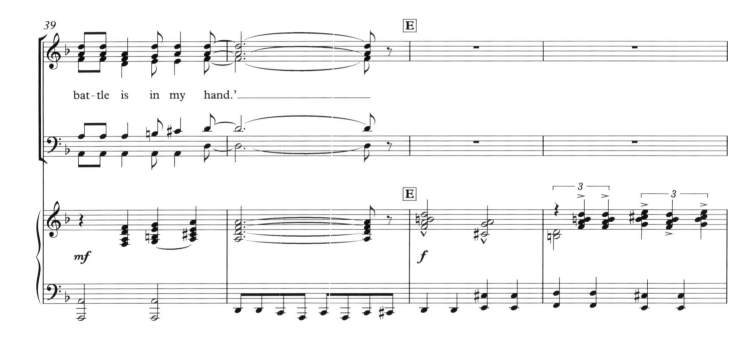

bat - tle is   in my   hand.'_____

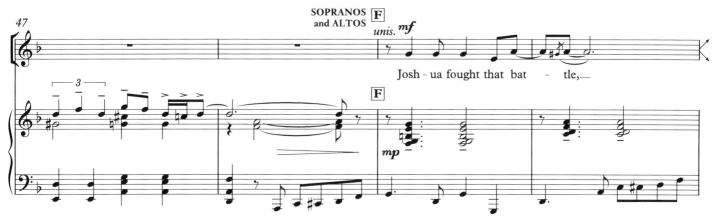

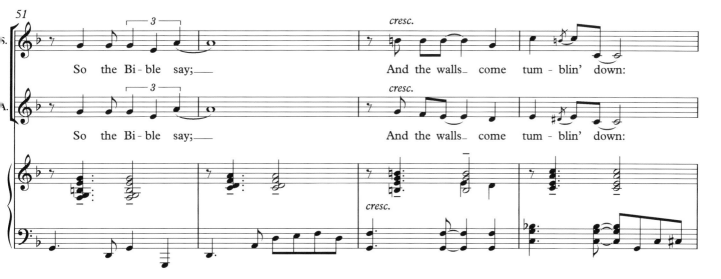

fit the bat-tle of Je-ri-cho, fit the bat-tle of Je-ri-cho,__ And the

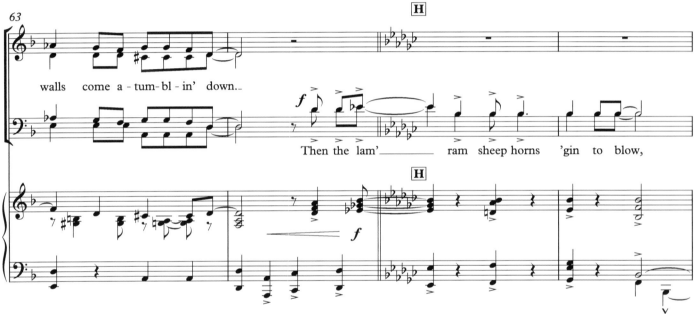

walls come a-tum-bl-in' down.__

Then the lam'_____ ram sheep horns 'gin to blow,

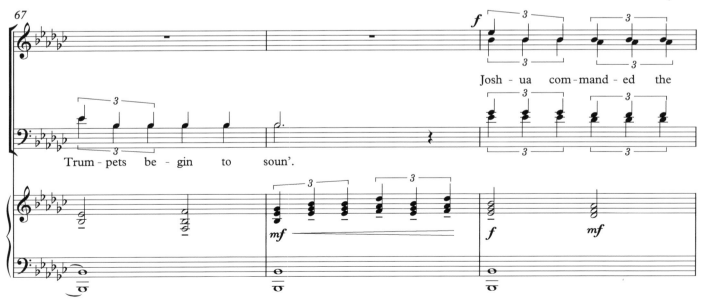

Trum-pets be-gin to soun'.

Josh-ua com-mand-ed the

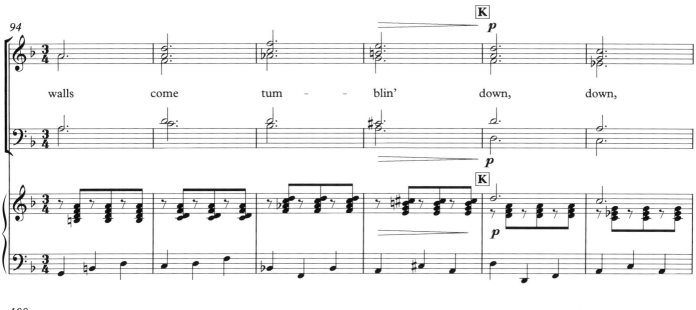

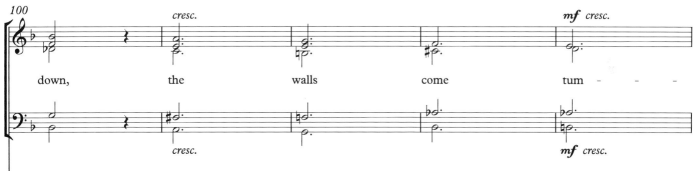

2. Steal away

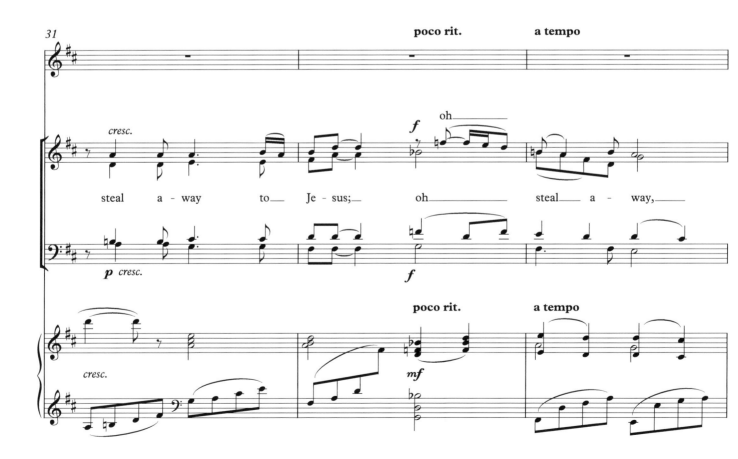

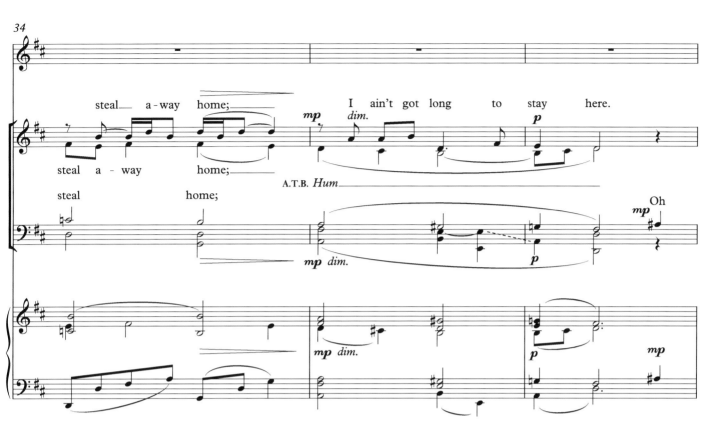

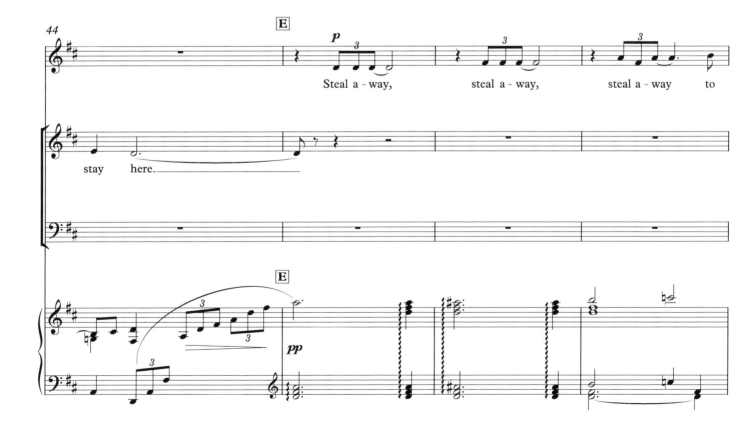

3. I got a robe

All of God's chil-dren got-ta shoes; When I get to hea-ven gon-na put on my shoes, Gon-na

hea - ven, hea - ven, hea - ven,

walk all ov - er God's hea-ven,— hea-ven,— hea-ven,—

Ev-'ry-bo-dy talk-in' 'bout hea-ven ain't go - ing there,
Hea - ven, hea-ven, and then I'm gon-na
Hea-ven, hea-ven,— gon-na

4. Sometimes I feel like a motherless child

Andante, with some freedom ♩ = 72

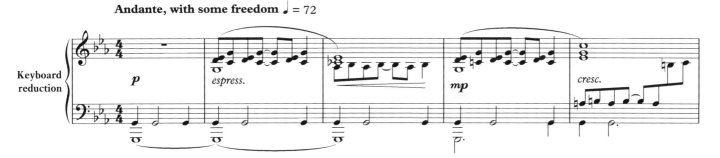

Some-times I feel like a mo-ther-less child, Some-times I feel like a mo-ther-less child,

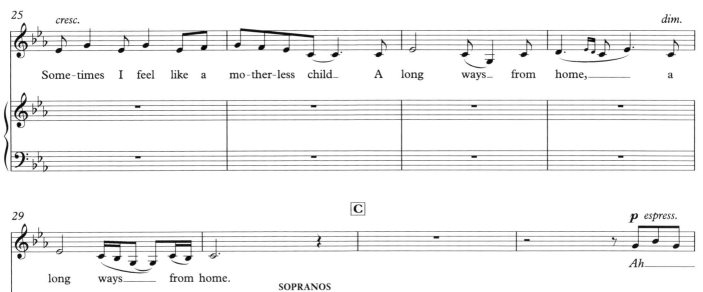

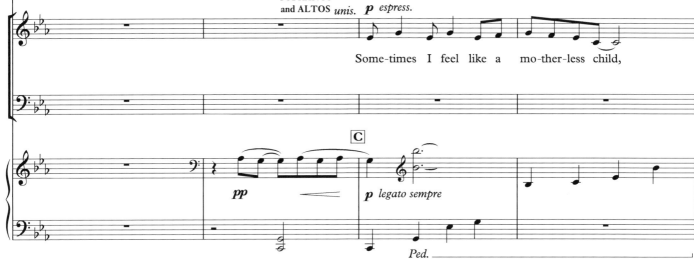

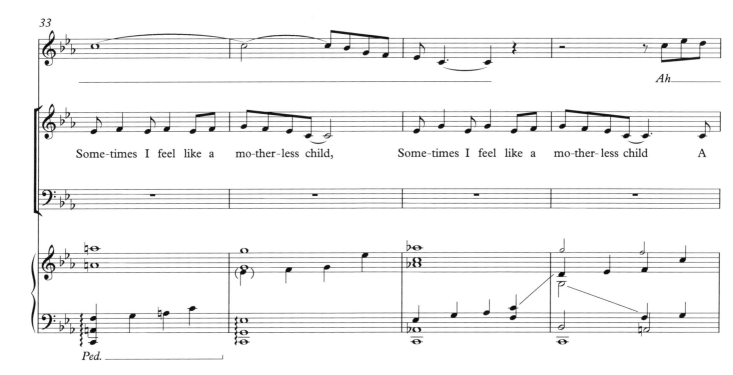

5. Ev'ry time I feel the spirit

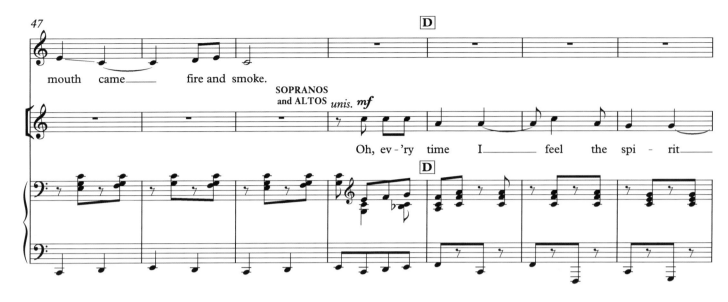

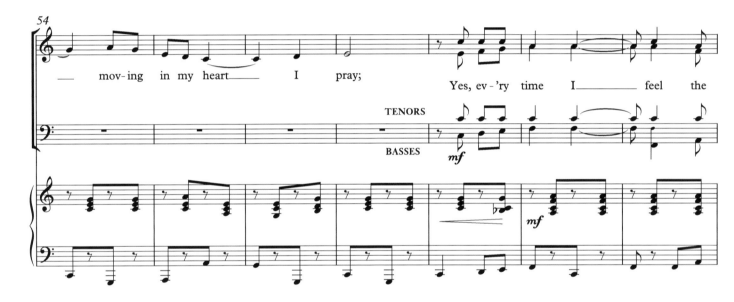

soul. And all a - round me looks so shine, I ask my

Lord if it all was mine.

6. Deep river

Deep_____ riv - er, Lord: I want to cross o-ver in-to camp ground._____

B

Oh, don't you want to go_____ to that Gos - pel_____ feast,_____ That

Oh,_____ don't you want to go to that Gos - pel feast,_____ That

Oh,_____ go to that

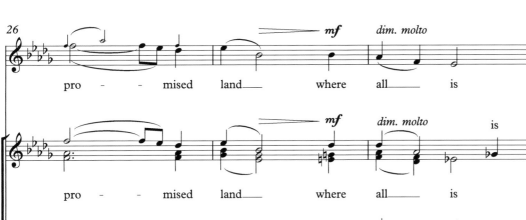

pro - - mised land___ where all___ is peace.___

Deep___ riv - er, my home is o - ver Jor - dan, Oh,

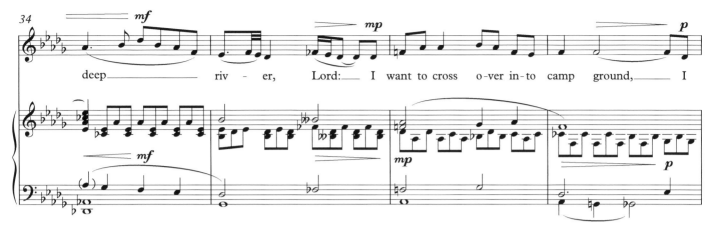

deep_____ riv - er, Lord:___ I want to cross o-ver in-to camp ground,___ I

D

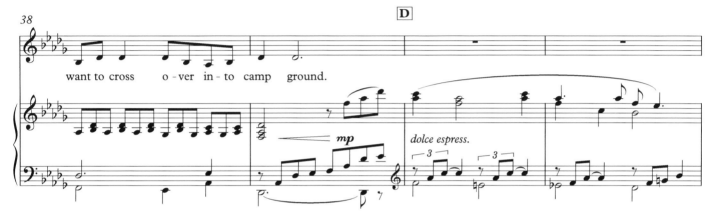

want to cross o - ver in - to camp ground.

rit. **E** a tempo

Deep_____ riv - er, my

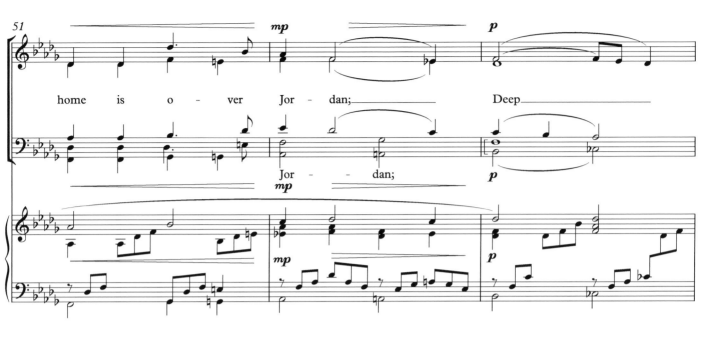

home is o - ver Jor - dan; Deep

Jor - dan;

SOLO

I want to cross____ o - ver in - to camp ground,

riv - er, Lord:

F

Lord, in - to camp ground, in - to

7. When the saints go marching in

Also available separately (978-0-19-343151-5)

46

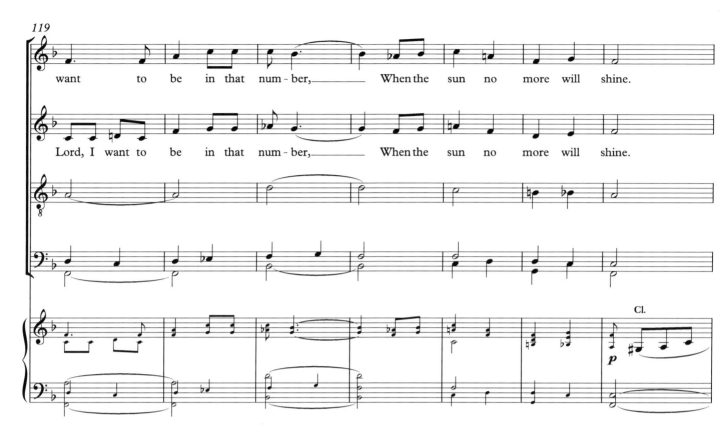

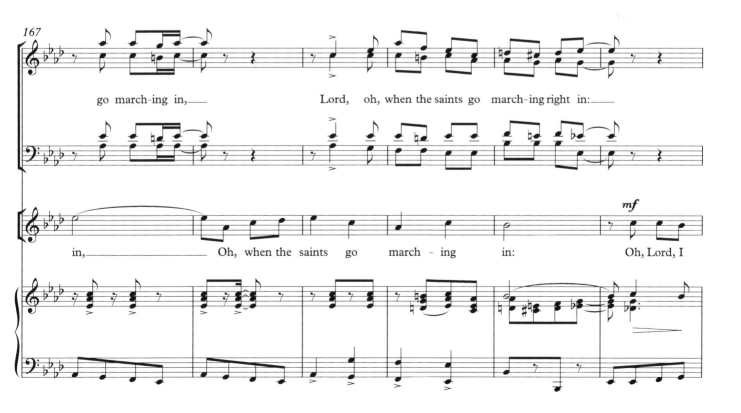